TRUE OR FALSE?

These things—maggots and a clock—have nothing in common.

Maggots and clocks have something major in common. They tell time!

That's right. Maggots and other bugs feast on rotting flesh. So the kinds of bugs on a dead body can help police figure out how long that person has been dead.

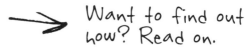 Want to find out how? Read on.

Book design: Red Herring Design/NYC

Library of Congress Cataloging-in-Publication Data
Denega, Danielle.
Gut-eating bugs : maggots reveal the time of death! / by Danielle Denega.
p. cm. — (24/7 : science behind the scenes)
Includes bibliographical references and index.
ISBN-13: 978-0-531-11824-5 (lib. bdg.)   978-0-531-17525-5 (pbk.)
ISBN-10: 0-531-11824-X (lib. bdg.)   0-531-17525-1 (pbk.)
1. Forensic entomology. 2. Death—Time of. 3. Criminal
investigation. I. Title.
RA1063.45D46 2007
614'.1—dc22   2006020871

GUT-EATING
BUGS

Maggots Reveal the Time of Death!

Danielle Denega

WARNING: All of the cases described in this book are real—and they all involve dead bodies covered in bugs!

Franklin Watts
A Division of Scholastic Inc.
New York • Toronto • London • Auckland • Sydney
Mexico City • New Delhi • Hong Kong
Danbury, Connecticut

CONTENTS

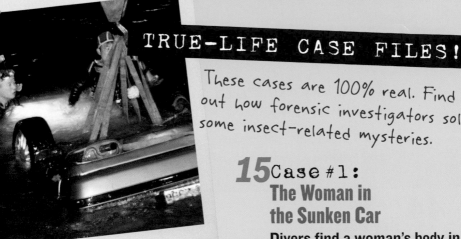

TRUE-LIFE CASE FILES!

These cases are 100% real. Find out how forensic investigators solved some insect-related mysteries.

A car is pulled from a river in Michigan.

15 Case #1:
The Woman in the Sunken Car
Divers find a woman's body in a sunken car. Only the bugs can tell how long she's been there.

25 Case #2:
A Family Tragedy
An entire family turns up dead in a cabin in the woods. Can flies help solve the mystery?

This cabin in Mississippi is the scene of a tragic murder.

35 Case #3:
The Case of the Grand Canyon Hikers
How did two hikers drown in a desert? Insects may hold the clue.

Two bodies are found in the Grand Canyon in Arizona.

FORENSIC DOWNLOAD

Don't bug out! Here's even more amazing stuff about forensic entomology.

Say a corpse is found in the woods. No one knows how long it's been there.

FORENSIC 411

That's a job for forensic entomologists. They'll study the insects on the corpse. That will help them figure out when the victim died.

IN THIS SECTION:

- how forensic entomologists REALLY TALK;
- how those SMALL INSECTS can help tell when a person died;
- and who else is at the CRIME SCENE.

What's the Buzz?

Forensic entomologists have their own way of speaking. Find out what their vocabulary means.

"I'm the expert in forensic entomology here. And I'd like to see the insect specimens from the body as soon as possible."

forensic entomology
(fuh-REN-zik EN-tow-MOLL-oh-gee) a science that uses bugs to find clues about when, and sometimes how, a person died

specimens
(SPESS-uh-muhns) samples or examples of something

"Entomo" means "having to do with insects." "Ology" means "the study of."

"The life cycle of a blowfly lasts almost two weeks. That means this guy's been dead awhile."

life cycle
(life SYE-kuhl) the series of changes a living thing goes through from birth to death

"Don't touch the corpse until the medical examiner gets here!"

corpse
(korps) a dead human body

Say What?

Here's some other lingo forensic entomologists might use on the job.

PMI
(PEE-em-eye) the time between when a person dies and when his or her body is found. It's short for *postmortem interval.*
"Boy, it looks like this corpse has been out in the woods for a long time. I'd estimate that the PMI is about 60 days."

"They're **maggots**—not snakes. Pick them up!"

maggots
(MAH-guts) the worm-like things that hatch from the eggs of flies. For some insects, they're also called larvae.

TOD
(TEE-oh-dee) the date and time when someone died. It's short for *time of death.*
"We'll nail down the TOD when we get the body back to the lab for testing."

"If you can finish this before the body decomposes, that would be great."

decompose
(dee-kuhm-POZE) to rot or decay

decomp
(DEE-komp) rot or decay. It's short for the word *decomposition.*
"Wow, this body smells! The decomp is really far along."

In open air, a corpse will attract **BLOWFLIES**. They lay thousands of eggs in the eyes, mouth, and nose of the body.

TIME AFTER DEATH
10 MINUTES

The blowfly eggs hatch, and **MAGGOTS** come out. The maggots feed on the body tissue.

TIME AFTER DEATH
12 HOURS

BEETLES are drawn to the body and eat the dry flesh.

TIME AFTER DEATH
24–36 HOURS

[And That's Not All]
Say a human body is left outside until it becomes a skeleton. In a moist, bug-friendly area, more than 300 species of insects will visit the corpse!

SPIDERS, MITES, and **MILLIPEDES** arrive and eat the bugs that are already on the corpse.

TIME AFTER DEATH
48 HOURS

These times are based on a body left outside in moderate weather.

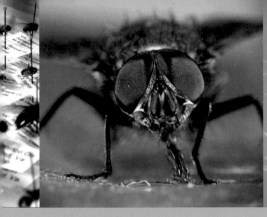
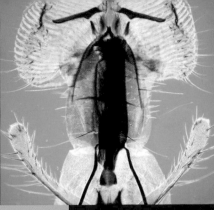

Bugging Out

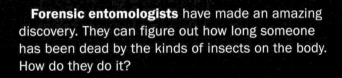

It's like clockwork. When there's a corpse outside, these insects always show up.

Forensic entomologists have made an amazing discovery. They can figure out how long someone has been dead by the kinds of insects on the body. How do they do it?

Who's There?

Entomologists take note of what *kinds* of bugs are on the body. That can help them figure out how long the **victim** has been dead. Insects arrive at bodies at predictable times. If there are beetles, for example, the body has been dead *at least* 24–36 hours.

What's the Life Cycle?

Entomologists also figure out what stage of development the insect is in. Every insect goes through predictable stages from birth to death. And scientists know about how long each of these stages takes. So if there's a fully grown blowfly, for example, that could mean that the body has been there 14 days!

What's the Weather?

Entomologists also have to consider the weather. Cold weather can slow down the life cycle of bugs. Hot weather can speed it up.

The Forensic Team

Forensic entomologists work as part of a team. Here's a look at some of the experts that help figure out how and when victims died.

FINGERPRINT EXAMINERS
They find, photograph, and collect fingerprints at the scene. Then, they compare them to prints they have on record.

METEOROLOGISTS
They collect information about the weather that might affect insect life cycles. They share the data with forensic entomologists.

FORENSIC TOXICOLOGISTS
They're called in to test victims for drugs, alcohol, and/or poison.

FORENSIC PATHOLOGISTS/ MEDICAL EXAMINERS
They're medical doctors who investigate suspicious deaths. They try to find out when and how someone died. They often direct other members of the team.

FORENSIC DENTISTS
They identify victims and criminals by their teeth or bitemarks.

FIRST RESPONDER POLICE OFFICERS/ DETECTIVES
They are often the ones to find, collect, and transport the evidence. They take photos and give the entomologists the crime scene data.

FORENSIC ENTOMOLOGISTS
They study the insects on or near a body. They use the information to figure out the PMI.

FORENSIC ANTHROPOLOGISTS
They're called in to identify victims by studying bones.

TRUE-LIFE CASE FILES!

24 hours a day, 7 days a week, 365 days a year, forensic entomologists are solving mysteries.

IN THIS SECTION:

▶ how an ENTOMOLOGIST figured out when a car (and a body) went into a river;

▶ how investigators caught a KILLER after six years, thanks in part to an insect;

▶ and how a forensic entomologist solved the MYSTERY of two people who drowned in the desert!

Here's how forensic entomologists get the job done.

What does it take to solve a crime? Good forensic entomologists don't just make guesses. They're scientists. They follow a step-by-step process.

As you read the case studies, you can follow along with them. Keep an eye out for the icons below. They'll clue you in to each step along the way.

 At the beginning of a case, forensic entomologists identify **one or two main questions** they have to answer.

 The next step is to **gather and analyze evidence**. Forensic entomologists collect as much information as they can. Then they study it to figure out what it means.

 Along the way, forensic entomologists come up with theories to explain what may have happened. They test these theories against the evidence. Does the evidence back up the theory? **If so, they've reached a conclusion**. And chances are they've come up with some important evidence that could help crack the case.

The Woman in the Sunken Car

Divers find a woman's body in a sunken car. Only the bugs can tell how long she's been there.

Muskegon River,
Western Michigan
June 23, 1989, 6:30 P.M.

Body Found!

Two divers find a car at the bottom of the river. And there's a woman's body inside!

On June 23, 1989, two scuba divers swam through the chilly waters of the Muskegon River in Michigan. When they reached the bottom, they discovered a terrible sight. A small red car lay upside down. Inside was the body of a dead woman.

The divers quickly reported their find. Police arrived on the scene and pulled the car out of the river. They lifted the woman's body from the car and considered the mystery. Had she been killed in an accident? Could she have been murdered? Police sent the body to the medical examiner, the **ME**, for an **autopsy**.

Meanwhile, officers took a careful look at the car. It was in decent condition. It didn't look like an accident had forced it into the river. Detectives decided it could have been pushed into the river from a nearby road.

But why was the woman trapped inside the car? When the autopsy report came in, police had part of

A medical examiner prepares to do an autopsy on a corpse. After the victim was found in the river, police ordered an autopsy.

On June 23, 1989, a car with a dead woman inside was found at the bottom of the Muskegon River in Michigan. Was this a terrible car crash—or a murder?

the answer. The victim's name was Hye-Yon Smith. Her injuries hadn't been caused by a car crash. She had been killed by blows to the head.

It was time to talk to the car's owner. An officer traced the license plates to David Smith, Hye-Yon's husband. Police decided to pay him a visit.

The Investigation Begins
When did Hye-Yon Smith really disappear?

David Smith had plenty to tell the police. His wife, Hye-Yon, had been missing for nine months. David claimed that on the night of September 30, 1988, he and Hye-Yon argued. She drove away angry into the foggy night. Two days later, he reported her missing. He hadn't heard from her since, he said.

However, when police questioned friends of the couple, they heard a different story. David told friends he had heard from Hye-Yon in January 1989.

That was strange. Why would David Smith lie about his wife's disappearance? David became the main **suspect** in the case.

Police began gathering **evidence**. They had one important question to answer: When did Hye-Yon die? If she was dumped in the river before January, then David had lied to his friends. That could help prove his guilt.

But figuring out the time of death wasn't going to be easy. The cold river water had **preserved** Hye-Yon's body. It hadn't **decayed** normally. The medical examiner couldn't use the rate of decay to figure out when she died.

Luckily, there were "witnesses" to the crime. When the car came up from the river, detectives noticed insects on the outside of the car. They collected specimens and saved them. Could the bugs help figure out when Hye-Yon died? This was a job for a forensic entomologist.

Aquatic insects live in the water. Some breathe through tiny gills. Others use strong hairs on their legs to push through the water, like little oars.

This is a great water beetle. This insect lives in lakes and ponds with muddy bottoms

Black Flies Don't Lie

How long had the car been in the river? Entomologist Richard Merritt decided to ask the bugs.

In July 1989, Dr. Richard Merritt received a delivery from detectives in charge of Hye-Yon Smith's case. Dr. Merritt is an entomologist at Michigan State University. His package contained bug specimens from David Smith's car.

Merritt knew his job. He had to use the insects to figure out when the car sunk in the river.

Merritt identified several types of insects. One find proved very useful: black fly **pupal casings**.

EVIDENCE

See the white stuff? That's a bunch of fly eggs. Fly larvae will hatch from these eggs.

Pupal casings are empty **cocoons** that have already released adult insects. These were the key to the case.

In Michigan, black flies lay eggs in the late spring or early summer. The eggs get buried in the dirt at the bottom of the river. They stop growing for a while. In the fall or early winter, they hatch into **larvae**. The larvae usually cling to rocks or plants and continue to grow. In this case, they attached themselves to a car.

Black fly larvae grow slowly in the winter water. After the snow melts, their growth speeds up. They form cocoons in late March or April. Finally, in May, the adult flies come out. They spend one or two months mating and laying eggs. Then they die.

A fully grown black fly on someone's skin. In Michigan, black flies usually come out in May and June—just in time to bother picnickers!

What did the black fly casings tell Dr. Merritt about Hye-Yon's time of death? When the car was found in June 1989, it held empty cocoons. The larvae inside had become flies and flown away.

THE CONCLUSION

That means that they must have been attached to the car by November or December 1988. David Smith claimed that Hye-Yon was alive in January 1989. According to the black flies, David was lying!

Dr. Merritt reported his findings to police. Detectives then felt they had the evidence they needed.

THE BLACK FLY TELLS ALL

**David Smith said his wife was alive in January.
Dr. Merritt said otherwise.**

Hye-Yon Smith's car was found on June 23, 1989. There were black fly casings on it. Dr. Merritt knew all about the life cycle of the black fly. The casings on Hye-Yon's car meant that black fly larvae had attached there by November or December 1988. And since the black fly is an **aquatic insect**, that meant that the car must have been underwater when the maggots showed up. That proved that Smith had been missing since November or December.

Here's the timeline.

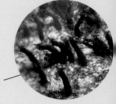

June 1988: Black flies near the Muskegon River lay their eggs.

November or December: Larvae hatch from the eggs and attach themselves to something in the river. In this case, they attach to the outside of the car.

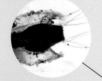

November–March 1989: The maggots grow very slowly during the winter.

March–April 1989: The larvae wrap themselves in cocoons. They **pupate**, or change into adults, inside these cocoons.

May 1989: Adult black flies come out of the cocoons. They leave empty casings on the car.

June 1989: The car is found. The adult black flies had left to lay their own eggs. The casings are still on the car.

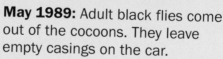

Case Closed

Dr. Merritt's understanding of the life cycle of the black fly helped send a murderer to jail.

On April 16, 1990, David Smith stood trial. The **prosecutor** claimed that David had killed Hye-Yon. David then put his wife's body in the car. He pushed the car into the river to make her death look like an accident.

Dr. Merritt testified as an **expert** witness. He said the pupal casings proved that the car had spent nearly nine months in the river.

Dr. Merritt in his lab. Here, he's looking through clothing for signs of insects.

A jury found David Smith guilty of killing his wife. He was sent to jail, thanks to one of the biggest pests in Michigan. As Dr. Merritt says, "The man was **convicted** of murder, based in part on the life cycle of an insect." 24/7

[Forensic Fact]
Black flies lay hundreds of eggs at a time!

Dr. Richard Merritt explains
what bugs have to say about death.

24/7: Why are insects so valuable in figuring out when someone died?

DR. MERRITT: Basically, insects do not lie! You can look at the temperatures the insects are exposed to. From that, you can calculate how big they should be or what stage they are in. This helps establish PMI—time between death and corpse discovery.

24/7: Why is weather important?

DR. MERRITT: It is important because insects are cold-blooded. That means they get their body temperature from their environment. So their growth is directly related to temperature. The higher the temperature, the faster they grow.

24/7: In the Muskegon River murder, flies helped solve the case. What other types of bugs are useful?

DR. MERRITT: Sometimes beetles can help. Beetles come in to feed on the dead person's dried skin. Beetle life cycles are longer than fly life cycles. If you find beetle larvae, you can figure out that the body has been dead for a while.

In the first case, insects helped to catch a suspect in a lie. But in the next case they seem to support what the suspect says. Or do they?

A Family Tragedy

Summit, Mississippi
May 1999

An entire family turns
up dead in a cabin in the
woods. Can some flies help
solve the mystery?

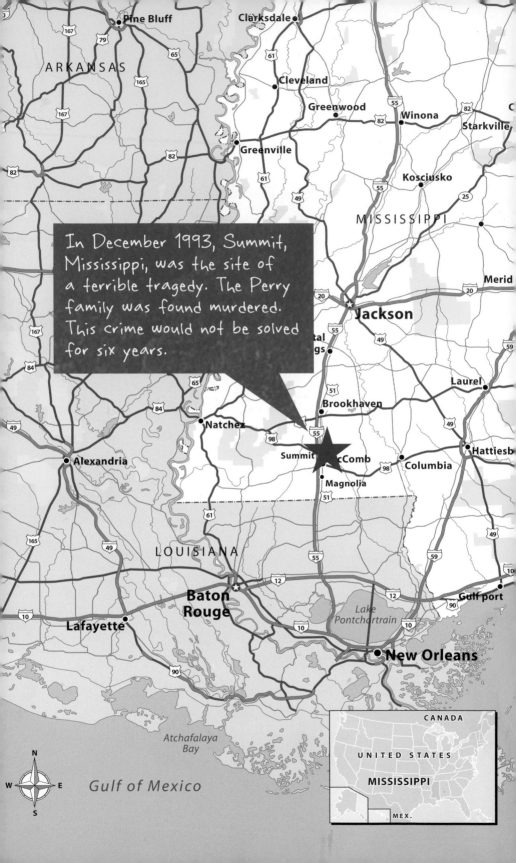

In December 1993, Summit, Mississippi, was the site of a terrible tragedy. The Perry family was found murdered. This crime would not be solved for six years.

Raising the Dead

**A six-year-old murder case is still unsolved.
Can crime scene photos reveal new information?**

In May 1999, Dr. William Bass got a call from a lawyer in Mississippi named Bill Goodwin. Dr. Bass was an expert in **forensic** science. Bill Goodwin needed his help.

Goodwin was working on a six-year-old murder case. In 1993, a husband, wife, and their daughter were found dead in a cabin. The bodies were badly decomposed.

The bodies of the Perry family were found in this cabin in December 1993.

Goodwin suspected that the stepfather of the murdered husband had committed the murders. But Goodwin didn't have any proof. What's more, the stepfather had a strong **alibi** for the two weeks before the bodies were found.

But what if the bodies had lain in the cabin longer than two weeks? That could make the stepfather's alibi worthless.

Now, all that was left of the crime scene were photos. Could Dr. Bass use these photos to figure out the PMI?

SOMETHING STINKS IN TENNESSEE

Researchers at the Body Farm study what happens to corpses as they decompose.

Ever heard of the Body Farm? The name is a little confusing. It's not exactly a farm. It's an outdoor field laboratory. And bodies don't grow there. They rot.

The Body Farm is a research lab at the University of Tennessee. Dr. William Bass started it in 1971. It's the only place where forensic experts can study real human bodies as they decay. Students, **FBI** agents, and others study there.

Students at the Body Farm learn to use the human body to solve crimes. They identify corpses by their teeth and bones. They determine the time and cause of death by a body's rate of decay.

In the early 1980s, Dr. Bass did one of the first forensic entomology studies there. He and a student watched a body decay. And they wrote down exactly when and where the bugs invaded.

Where does the Body Farm get its bodies? Medical examiners often send unclaimed corpses there. Some people even decide to give their bodies to the lab after they die.

Today, there are almost 400 bodies being studied on the farm.

Dr. William Bass talks to reporters about his work at the Body Farm. There, he and other scientists study how dead bodies decay.

Murder in the Making

In 1993, something terrible happened to the Perry family.

Goodwin's case had a gruesome story behind it. On December 16, 1993, a man named Michael Rubenstein called the sheriff. Rubenstein owned a cabin near the town of Summit. For the past six weeks, his stepson Daryl Perry had been staying at the cabin with his wife, Annie, and their four-year-old daughter, Krystal.

Rubenstein had just gone to visit them. When he opened the door, he found the family dead.

The police investigated, and Rubenstein became their main suspect. They found out that he held a life-insurance policy on his granddaughter, Krystal. The day after the bodies were discovered, Rubenstein filed a claim—for $250,000.

But there was no evidence to link Rubenstein to the crime. He had an alibi for December 2–16. He also had a witness. Rubenstein's niece claimed that she had seen Annie Perry alive on December 2.

For six years, the murders went unsolved.

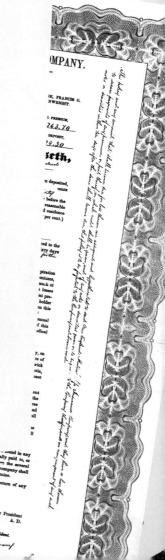

The Bugs Speak

What can the maggots in the police photos tell Dr. Bass about the crime?

Then in 1999, Goodwin called Dr. Bass. During the original investigation, there was a question about the victims' time of death. Now Goodwin was hoping that Bass would be able to figure that out.

If Bass discovered that Annie had died before December 2, 1993, that would mean that Rubenstein's niece had lied. That would also mean that Rubenstein's alibi was no good.

Two days after Goodwin's call, the crime scene photos arrived at Dr. Bass's office. Dr. Bass took them out and got to work. He studied the images under a magnifying glass. The bodies were badly decomposed and covered with maggots.

Dr. Bass looked at weather information for the area around Summitt. At warm temperatures, maggots can eat most of the flesh on a body in two weeks. But it had been cold during November and December 1993. The temperature sunk below freezing on eight nights. At those temperatures, a body would decay more slowly.

Dr. Bass compared his evidence with research he had done at the Body Farm.

Check out the life cycle of a blowfly on pages 48–49.

THE CONCLUSION !

He concluded that the bodies had been dead for 25 to 35 days before they were found.

Still, one thing troubled Dr. Bass. The bugs on the bodies refused to support his conclusion. He measured the maggots in the photos. Most of them were about a ½ inch (1.3 cm) long. In the cold weather, it had probably taken them two weeks to grow to that stage. Bass couldn't prove that they had been there any earlier.

If the Perrys had been dead longer than two weeks, there should be other insect evidence on the bodies. The maggots should have formed cocoons. Inside the cocoons, they would have transformed into flies. The flies would have broken free and flown away. They would have left behind empty cocoons, or pupal casings. Why couldn't Dr. Bass find any pupal casings?

Dr. Bass was still convinced he was right about the time of death. But without pupal casings, would he be able to convince a jury?

The maggots from the photo were two weeks old. But Dr. Bass thought the victims had been dead longer than that.

The Trial

Dr. Bass thought the victims had been dead for a month. So why were the maggots only two weeks old?

In June 1999, Dr. Bass drove to Mississippi for Michael Rubenstein's trial. He testified that the bodies had been decomposing for a month. He did his best to explain his theory to the jury. But he could only conclude one thing without a doubt. The bodies had only hosted maggots for two weeks.

In the end, the jury couldn't decide. The judge ordered a new trial for January 2000. Dr. Bass had six months to prepare.

In January, Dr. Bass took the stand again. This time he was ready. He admitted he hadn't found any pupal casings. But there were reasons for that, he said. Blow flies don't move at temperatures below 54°F (12°C). The cold probably slowed them down. In addition, the cabin was tightly sealed. That made it harder for the flies to smell the corpses. The Perrys had probably been dead for days before the first blowfly found them.

Would this explanation convince a jury? Dr. Bass wasn't sure.

BUG PROOF

If Dr. Bass was right, Rubenstein didn't have an alibi for the day of the Perrys' murder.

November 8, 1993: The Perrys went to the cabin.

November 15: According to Dr. Bass, this is when the Perrys were killed.

December 2–16: This is the time period for which Rubenstein had an alibi. He was out of town.

December 16: Rubenstein discovered the bodies.

Casings Revealed

Dr. Bass spots something in an autopsy photo. Will it prove that he was right all along?

These are pupal casings like the one Dr. Bass saw in the photo. Casings can be as small as grains of rice.

After Dr. Bass spoke, another expert took the stand. She had examined the bodies in 1993, when they were first discovered. She showed the courtroom a series of autopsy photos. These photos had been enlarged. Tiny details were visible to the naked eye.

Dr. Bass took a long look from his seat in the courtroom. These photos were new to him. A close-up of Krystal Perry's head caught his eye. And there it was. It was something he had been hoping to see for six months.

In the roots of Krystal's hair were brown specks the size of grains of rice. They were pupal casings.

Dr. Bass whispered his discovery to Bill Goodwin. Goodwin approached the judge. They agreed to put Dr. Bass back on the witness stand.

Dr. Bass told the jury what the empty cocoons proved. Blowfly eggs had been on those bodies for longer than two weeks. Rubenstein's niece could not have seen Annie on December 2. The Perrys were already dead. And Rubenstein could have killed them.

Case Closed

Michael Rubenstein is convicted, thanks in part to a few insects.

On February 3, 2000, the jury found Michael Rubenstein guilty of first-degree murder. They believed he had planned the Perry murders. They gave him life sentences for killing Daryl and Annie. For young Krystal, they felt he deserved worse. She was just a child. And Rubenstein had murdered her for money. For that, he got the death penalty.

Bill Bass wrote about the case in a book called *Death's Acre*. In it he wonders how a man could commit such a crime. "Every murder is ... brutal," he says, "but this case was especially shocking." That made his work even more satisfying than usual. "If my expertise can help put away even one [killer] like that, then all my years of study and research have been well spent." 24/7

In this case, cold weather and sealed doors confused investigators. But in the next case, bugs and a weather report helped to clear things up.

The Case of the Grand Canyon Hikers

How did two hikers drown in a desert? Insects may hold the clue.

Bodies Found!

Two hikers have been found dead in the desert. It seems like they *drowned*. How could that be?

On August 26, 1992, two hikers made an unexpected discovery in the Grand Canyon. They were hiking the Tonto Trail, on the north rim. It was hot and dry. Temperatures in northern Arizona often reach 100°F (38°C) in the summer.

The hikers wandered a ½ mile (.8 km) off the trail. At the base of a cliff, they found two dead bodies. One belonged to a man, the other to a woman. They lay about 100 feet (30 m) apart. The woman had a homemade splint on her leg. Aside from that, there was little sign of injury. What could have happened?

The hikers got in touch with police as soon as they could. At 6:30 that evening, a helicopter flew the bodies out of the canyon. The two corpses were sent to the Medical Examiner's Office in Flagstaff, Arizona.

The next day, the ME performed autopsies. The results were bizarre. The couple had drowned. It didn't make sense. The bodies were found

The bodies of two hikers were found near a trail in the Grand Canyon.

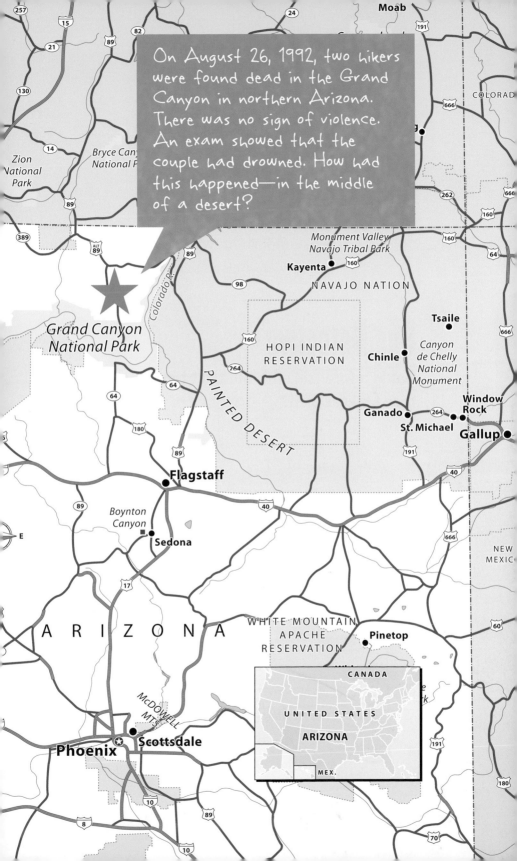

On August 26, 1992, two hikers were found dead in the Grand Canyon in northern Arizona. There was no sign of violence. An exam showed that the couple had drowned. How had this happened—in the middle of a desert?

in a dry, desert area. How could they have drowned?

Investigators needed more information. Most important, when did the couple die? For the answer, they called a forensic entomologist.

Bug Detective

Could a forensic entomologist figure out when these hikers died?

The agent in charge of the case called Dr. M. Lee Goff. Dr. Goff is a forensic entomologist. He works at Chaminade University in Hawaii. Lucky for Dr. Goff, the agent knew something about **entomology**. He'd been trained in collecting insects. He had already collected specimens from the corpses. Dr. Goff had him go back and get soil samples from the site. The evidence arrived in Hawaii on August 31.

Dr. Goff's mission was clear. He needed to figure out when the hikers died.

To do that, he'd have to study the insect evidence.

Go to page 50 to find out more about the Berlese funnel.

His first job was to identify the specimens. He started by putting the soil samples into a **Berlese funnel**. The funnel forces bugs out of soil and dead leaves. They fall into a liquid that keeps them from rotting. Then they can be examined under a microsope.

Dr. Goff took a close look at his bugs. He identified several types of flies, beetles, and mites. He thought that one type of larva was that of a fly called the screw worm.

But Dr. Goff needed to see the adult fly to be certain. So, he stuck the maggots in a warm place. In a few days they formed cocoons. When the adult flies came out, Dr. Goff knew he was right. They were screw worm flies. These flies held the key to the case.

Weather was the next piece of the puzzle. Dr. Goff needed to know exact temperatures in the canyon during the days before August 26. Heat would have made his screw worms grow faster. Cold would have slowed them down. Weather stations in the canyon provided the information.

One of the insects Dr. Goff found was the screw worm. The screw worm maggot is in the top photo. The screw worm adult fly is below that.

39

A meteorologist checks the weather patterns. A weather report provided Dr. Goff with important information.

Dr. Goff put all his data together. The bodies had been out in the open. Temperatures had been warm. Flies must have found the bodies quickly and laid their eggs. Screw worms hatched within a day. Judging from their size, they had grown on the body for another four days.

THE CONCLUSION

Dr. Goff came to a conclusion. The couple must have died five days before they were found.

He placed the time of death on the evening of August 21. This fit with information the agents in Arizona had collected. The hikers had been last seen alive on August 18. They must have died a few days after that. But how?

Drowned in a Desert

Dr. Goff knew when the couple had died.
Could he also figure out how?

Dr. Goff had figured out the time of death. Now he turned his attention to the cause. There were still a few mysteries. Why were the hikers found 100 feet apart? How did they drown? And had someone moved the bodies?

Once again, weather data gave Dr. Goff the answers. On the evening of August 21, a heavy rainfall hit the area. The downpours caused **flash floods** in the canyon.

Now, the pieces of the puzzle came together. It seemed that the woman had fallen and hurt her leg. Her hiking partner climbed to help her. They made a splint for the woman's leg. But by that time it was dark. The two hikers were stuck on the bottom of the canyon for the night.

A flash flood is a flood that takes place very suddenly. Large amounts of water move in, and quickly move out again—in a flash!

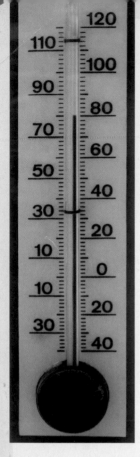

The morning after the flash flood, the canyon warmed up. The flood waters evaporated.

That's when flood waters filled the canyon. Flash floods often happen dangerously fast. The two hikers didn't have time to escape. They drowned in the flood. Rushing waters swept their bodies down the canyon. It left them 100 feet apart.

The sun came up the next morning. Temperatures rose. The flood waters quickly **evaporated** in the heat. By this time, bugs had already begun their feast. In time they would tell the secret of the deaths. The two hikers had, in fact, drowned in a desert. 24/7

THE TRAGIC HIKE

What happened to the hikers? Here's what Dr. Goff learned from the bugs.

August 18, 1992: Hikers last seen alive.

August 21: There's a flash flood in the canyon. Hikers drown.

August 22: Flood dries up. Screw flies lay eggs on the hikers' bodies.

August 23: Screw flies hatch and become larvae. Larvae grow August 23, 24, 25, and 26.

August 26: Hikers' bodies discovered. Screw worm larvae found on the bodies.

FORENSIC DOWNLOAD

Here's even more amazing stuff about forensic entomology for you to buzz about.

IN THIS SECTION:

- ▶ how bugs helped to CATCH A MURDERER—in 1235;
- ▶ how FORENSIC ENTOMOLOGY has been in the news;
- ▶ the TOOLS that are used to study bugs;
- ▶ and whether forensic entomology might be in YOUR FUTURE!

1235 Flies Catch Murderer

What's the first use of insect evidence on record? In China, someone was killed in a slashing attack. The murder weapon? A **sickle**. A clever judge ordered all villagers to meet—and bring their sickles. The tools all looked clean. But flies swarmed one of them. The flies could detect blood. They led the judge to the murderer!

Key Dates in Forensic

How did people figure out that insects could hold the secrets of the dead? It all started in China in the 1200

1963 What a Pig!

Entomologist Jerry Payne studied decomposing pigs. He recorded which bugs showed up when. Not many people need to know exactly when their pigs die. But pigs decay at the same rate as humans. So, Payne's data was useful to forensic scientists.

[Poison Detectors]

If a person has been poisoned, the poison will appear in the maggots that eat the body. Police can use this as evidence!

1668 Where Do Maggots Come From?

For centuries people have seen flies and maggots on rotting flesh. But until 1668, no one connected the two pests. Most people thought maggots actually grew from the dead flesh. A scientist named Francesco Redi finally cleared things up. He discovered that the maggots came from eggs laid by the flies.

1850 Pupae Appear in Court

A French doctor used bugs for evidence at a trial. In the spring of 1850, the body of a baby was found in a house near Paris. The couple living in the house became suspects. Dr. Bergeret d'Arbois found fly **pupae** on the body. He concluded they came from eggs laid in 1848—before the suspects moved in. The doctor's calculations were probably wrong. But the couple got off the hook.

Entomology

1981 Bugs on the Body Farm

Dr. William Bass and Bill Rodriguez performed the first entomological study done at the Body Farm. They recorded the stages at which insects appear on rotting *human* bodies.

2000 On the Small Screen

TV shows about solving crimes, like *CSI*, make forensic entomologists into celebrities—well, almost!

In the News

Read all about it! Forensic entomology is swarming all over the news!

Blowflies Infest Museum!

BERKELEY, CALIFORNIA—
February 2006

Forensic entomologist Dr. Lee Goff has designed a new museum exhibit in Berkeley, California. The exhibit is called CSI: Crime Scene Insects. It shows how bugs can be used to help solve crimes.

The exhibit features some pretty gross stuff—like pictures of corpses and the blowflies that love them. One 14-year-old boy admitted that he liked the show. "Once you get over the gross factor, it's pretty interesting," he said. "It's definitely standable."

Top: Dr. Lee Goff is an expert witness at many trials. Here, he explains bugs to a jury in July 2002. *Below:* Dr. Goff's souvenirs from solving crimes.

In March 2001, Professor Gail Anderson appeared in *Time* magazine. She was selected as one of the six leaders in the field of crime and punishment.

New Lab Uses Bugs to Solve Crimes!

BRITISH COLUMBIA, CANADA—
March 19, 2001

Entomology professor Gail Anderson poses in her lab at the Simon Fraser University in Canada. In September 2000, Anderson's university opened the first lab founded to study how insects can help solve crimes.

In addition to her work at the university, Anderson helps police solve crimes involving insects. In the past 12 years, she has assisted with more than 130 murder investigations. Anderson is passionate about her work. "The dead have rights, too," she says.

What's going on at the Simon Fraser University in Canada? There, insect experts are figuring out how to solve crime.

Bugs R Us

Have a look at the tools, equipment, forms, and other stuff used by forensic entomologists.

A FLY'S LIFE

Scientists use the life cycle of bugs to figure out how long a body has been dead.

Blowflies are usually the first creatures to find a corpse. By the time police arrive, the flies have moved in. They've laid their eggs. The eggs may have hatched into maggots. The maggots may have built cocoons.

Forensic entomologists know exactly when these stages happen. (They vary depending on the temperature.) They use the information to estimate the time of death.

Maggots are the worm-like things that hatch from eggs. They're also called larvae.

Minutes after death: Adult blowflies arrive and lay their eggs.

23 hours: The eggs hatch into larvae, or maggots. At this stage they're called first instar maggots.

2 days: The larvae grow, turning into second instar maggots.

8 days: The maggots wrap themselves in cocoons. This is called the pupa stage.

The cocoon is the covering spun by larvae during the pupal stage.

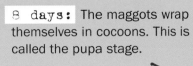

3 days: The larvae turn into third instar maggots and start to move around.

The pupa is the form of the blowfly when it's in the cocoon.

14 days: Adult blowflies come out of the cocoon. They find another corpse to call home. They lay their eggs, and the whole life cycle starts again!

[Watch the Weather]

Flies are sensitive to heat and cold. That means forensic entomologists have to know the weather. Cold weather slows the life cycle down. Warm weather speeds it up. The life cycle on this page is based on a nice, comfortable 70°F (21°C).

TOOLS AND EQUIPMENT

insect net Flies are caught using a common insect net. Insect nets are made so that the little insects can't escape.

forceps Beetles are collected from the crime scene using forceps. Forceps are a tool that you use to pick something up. They're sort of like the tweezers shown here. Entomologists use forceps with small tips so that they don't crush the insect specimens.

spoon A spoon is used to scoop up maggots from the scene.

latex gloves An entomologist wears latex gloves when handling insect evidence.

trowel
A trowel is used for collecting soil and leaf-litter samples and searching for buried larvae and pupa.

Berlese funnel Many bugs prefer to live in moist, cool conditions and rarely leave the cover of dead leaves. A Berlese funnel is a trap that works by heating up the temperature of leaf litter. That forces the bugs out. As a light bulb in the trap warms up the plant material, the insects seek a cooler, wetter place to hide. Then the insects fall into the trap!

microscope Insects are studied up-close under a microscope. A microscope is a scientific tool that has a lens that you look through. The lens makes things seem larger than they are. That helps scientists see details of small insects.

labels It is very important that the insects from the scene are carefully labeled. Labels are written with a dark pencil or pen with waterproof ink.

killing jar and ethyl acetate Insect samples are put into a glass container called a killing jar. A killing jar is a device used by entomologists to kill captured insects quickly without damaging them. Inside the jar are cotton balls or plaster soaked with ethyl acetate. (That's just fingernail polish remover.) That kills the specimens.

paintbrush A paintbrush with very fine bristles is moistened and then used for collecting eggs.

ENTOMOLOGY FORM

On forms like this one, entomologists record what specimens were collected and when and where they were found.

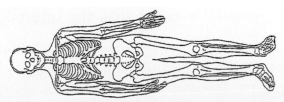

Scene temperatures: ambient:_____ ambient (1ft) _____ body surface_____
ground surface_____ under-body interface_____ maggot mass_____
water temp, if aquatic_____ enclosed structure_____ AC/Heat- on/off_____
ceiling fan- on/off_____ soil temperature- 10cm_____ 20cm_____
Number of preserved samples _____ Number of live samples _____
NOTE: Record all temperatures periodically each day at the site for 3-5 days after body recovery.

HELP WANTED:
Forensic
Entomologist

Interested in the world of insects? Here's more information about the field.

Dr. John Wallace is an entomologist in Pennsylvania.

24/7: How did you become interested in entomology?

DR. WALLACE: My father was a biology teacher, and he introduced me to the wonderful world of insects.

24/7: Did you always know that you wanted to do this as a career?

DR. WALLACE: What I did know was that I would work in biology. And if I could pay the bills as an entomologist, then that would be it.

24/7: How did you get into the forensic side?

DR. WALLACE: My major professor in graduate school, Dr. Rich Merritt, asked me to assist him with a murder case. He also asked me to help teach a forensic entomology course. Now I teach my own courses. I also work cases in various states. And I specialize in cases involving aquatic insects.

24/7: What's the most difficult part of your job?

DR. WALLACE: Every case is challenging and requires a great deal of focus and thought. On death scene investigations, cases involving children are always difficult to experience. Another difficult thing about my job is that people believe what they see on TV shows. TV shows aren't always entirely clear about what forensic entomologists do.

24/7: What part of your job do you enjoy the most?

DR. WALLACE: When I can help solve a case.

24/7: What advice would you give young people who are interested in forensic entomology?

DR. WALLACE: You need to be observant. Pay attention to detail. Have a creative mind. You also have to keep trying when situations are difficult. Also, work hard in math, biology, and earth sciences, such as meteorology.

24/7: Is there anything else you'd like to add?

DR. WALLACE: We have formed a new society called the North American Forensic Entomology Association. Young people are encouraged to join and learn about what we do.

THE STATS

DAY JOB
Most forensic entomologists work in labs. Or they're professors at colleges. They are not full-time crime scene investigators. They're called to crime scenes when they're needed.

MONEY
The average salary for a forensic entomology professor is $70,000–$100,000 a year. They are paid a few hundred dollars per case for their investigative work.

EDUCATION
Forensic entomologists must finish the following:
▶ 4 years of college
▶ 4 years of graduate school in medical entomology

THE NUMBERS
There are only about 62 forensic entomologists in the world.

DO YOU HAVE WHAT IT TAKES?

Take this totally unscientific quiz to see if forensic entomology might be a good career for you.

1 Do you like to be outside?
a) Yes, I go hiking a lot.
b) Yes, but I hate hot weather
c) I only like nature TV shows.

2 Are you interested in science, like biology?
a) I read everything I can find about science.
b) I think it's sort of interesting.
c) I'm only interested in my next meal.

3 Are you patient about finding answers?
a) Yes, I just want to find out the truth.
b) Most of the time.
c) No, I want an answer right away!

4 Do you get grossed out by bugs?
a) Nope. I like looking at bugs and am not afraid to be near them.
b) I don't mind them.
c) I feel sick just thinking about that question.

5 How do you feel about helping to put criminals in jail?
a) I really want to fight crime.
b) I think crime-solving is sort of interesting.
c) Leave me out of it.

YOUR SCORE

Give yourself 3 points for every "**a**" you chose. Give yourself 2 points for every "**b**" you chose. Give yourself 1 point for every "**c**" you chose.

If you got **13–15 points**, you'd probably be a good forensic entomologist. If you got **10–12 points**, you might be a good forensic entomologist. If you got **5–9 points**, you might want to look at another career!

HOW TO GET STARTED...NOW!

It's never too early to start working toward your goals.

GET AN EDUCATION

▶ Focus on your science classes, such as earth science and biology.

▶ Start thinking about college. Look for ones with good entomology programs.

▶ Read the newspaper. Keep up with what's going on in your community.

▶ Read anything you can find about forensic entomology.

▶ Research scholarships, such as the BioQuip Undergraduate Scholarship and the Stan Beck Fellowship.

▶ Graduate from high school!

NETWORK!

Find out about forensic groups in your area. See if you can find a local entomologist who might be willing to give you advice.

GET AN INTERNSHIP

▶ Look for an internship with an entomologist.

▶ Join entomology associations that encourage young people, like the American Academy of Forensic Sciences Young Forensic Scientist's Forum.

LEARN ABOUT OTHER JOBS IN ENTOMOLOGY

Regular entomologists who do not work in crime scenes are also professors. They can also work for federal government agencies such as the U.S. Department of Defense and Centers for Disease Control. They can also work for mosquito control agencies, the United Nations, the World Bank, and the World Health Organization.

Resources

Looking for more information about forensic entomology Here are some resources you don't want to miss!

PROFESSIONAL ORGANIZATIONS

American Academy of Forensic Sciences (AAFS)
www.aafs.org
410 North 21st Street
Colorado Springs, CO 80904-2798
PHONE: 719-636-1100
FAX: 719-636-1993

The AAFS is a professional society dedicated to the application of science to the law. They promote education and accuracy in the forensic sciences.

American Board of Forensic Entomology (ABFE)
www.research.missouri.edu/
entomology
FOR MORE INFORMATION ON
ABFE CERTIFICATION CONTACT:
Richard W. Merritt, PhD
Department of Entomology
Michigan State University
East Lansing, MI 48824
PHONE: 517-355-8309
FAX: 517-353-4354

The ABFE is a professional organization that certifies entomologists. To receive the status as Diplomate, the ABFE requires you to have a PhD and experience.

Entomological Society of America (ESA)
www.entsoc.org/index.htm
10001 Derekwood Lane, Suite 100
Lanham, MD 20706-4876
PHONE: 301-731-4535
FAX: 301-731-4538
EMAIL: esa@entsoc.org

The ESA is the largest organization in the world serving the professional and scientific needs of entomologists and people in related disciplines. Founded in 1889, it has more than 5,700 members from educational institutions, health agencies, private industry, and government.

North American Forensic Entomology Association (NAFEA)
www.nafea.net

The NAFEA aims to promote the development of forensic entomology throughout North America and to encourage cooperation with other organizations.

BOOKS ABOUT ENTOMOLOGY AND FORENSIC SCIENCE

Bass, Dr. Bill, and Jon Jefferson. *Death's Acre: Inside the Legendary Forensic Lab, the Body Farm.* New York: Putnam, 2003.

Byrd, Jason H., and James L. Castner, eds. *Forensic Entomology: The Utility of Arthopiods in Legal Investigations.* Boca Raton, Fla.: CRC, 2000.

Goff, M. Lee. *A Fly for the Prosecution: How Insect Evidence Helps Solve Crimes.* Cambridge, Mass.: Harvard University Press, 2001.

Innes, Brian. *The Search for Forensic Evidence.* Milwaukee: Gareth Stevens, 2005.

WEB SITES

A link to an interview with
Dr. Robert D. Hall about
being a forensic entomologist:
**www.entsoc.org/resources/
education/hall.htm**

A link to an interview with
Dr. M. Lee Goff about
being a forensic entomologist:
**www.csicollection.com/
interview04.php**

Court TV article
www.crimelibrary.com/criminal_mi
nd/forensics/anthropology/6.html

Discovery Channel article
dsc.discovery.com/fansites/
onthecase/toolbox/tool_05.html

National Geographic article
news.nationalgeographic.com/
news/2004/04/0423_040423_tvb
ugman.html

**Natural History
Museum article**
www.nhm.ac.uk/nature-online/
science-of-natural-history/
forensic-sleuth/fathommaggot2/
on-maggots-and-murders-
forensic-entomology.html

Forensicentomology.com
This Web site contains lots of
information about entomology.
There's even a section to
submit cases.
**http://www.forensicentomology.
com/index.html**

Forensic Entomology Exhibit
An awesome traveling forensic
entomology exhibit called CSI: Crime
Scene Insects is making its way
around the country. See **www.
csi-exhibit.com/features.html**
for more information and a
schedule of dates in your area!

A video about forensic entomology
called **Crime Scene Creatures**
**www.shopthirteen.org/webapp/wc
s/stores/servlet/ProductDisplay?pr
oductId=42754&storeId=10552&ca
talogId=10101&langId=-1**

A

alibi (AL-uh-bye) *noun* proof that you were somewhere else when a crime happened

anthropologist (an-THRO-pol-oh-jist) *noun* someone who studies humans, including their bones, language, and culture

aquatic insect (uh-KWA-tik IN-sekt) *noun* an insect that lives on top of or in the water for a large part of its life

autopsy (AW-top-see) *noun* an exam done on a dead person to figure out how he or she died

B

Berlese funnel (BUHRL-eese FUN-nuhl) *noun* a tool used to remove insects from leaves and dirt

C

cocoon (KUH-koon) *noun* the covering spun by the larvae of an insect. The cocoon acts as a covering for the pupal stage.

convict (kuhn-VIKT) *verb* to find someone guilty of a crime

corpse (KORPS) *noun* a dead body

D

decay (dih-KAY) *verb* to rot

decomp (DEE komp) *noun* rottenness. It's short for the word *decomposition*.

decompose (dee-kuhm-POZE) *verb* to rot

E

entomology (EN-tow-moll-oh-gee) *noun* the study of bugs, including their life cycles and behaviors

entomologist (EN-tow-moll-oh-jist) *noun* someone who studies bugs, including their life cycles and behaviors

ethyl acetate (ETH-ell ASS-uh-tayte) *noun* a chemical similar to fingernail polish remover used to kill insects

evaporate (i-VAP-uh-rate) *verb* to change from a liquid to a gas or vapor

Dictionary

evidence (EHV-un-denss) *noun* things that help prove that someone is guilty or innocent

expert (ex-purt) *noun* someone who knows a lot about a subject. For a list of forensic experts, see page 12.

F

FBI (EF-bee-eye) *noun* a part of the U.S. government that investigates major crimes. It stands for *Federal Bureau of Investigation.*

flash flood (FLASH fluhd) *noun* a flood that takes place very suddenly. Large amounts of water move in, and then quickly move out again. A flash flood is usually caused by lots of rain in a short period of time.

forensic (fuh-REN-sik) *adjective* a kind of science used to help investigate crimes

forensic entomologist (fuh-REN-sik EN-tow-moll-oh-jist) *noun* a scientist who uses insects to find find clues about when, and sometimes how, a person died

forensic entomology (fuh-REN-sik EN-tow-moll-oh-gee) *noun* a science that uses bugs to find clues about when, and sometimes how, a person died

K

killing jar (KIHL-ling jar) *noun* a glass jar used to store insect specimens

L

larva (LAR-vuh) *noun* the form of an insect that hatches from the egg. More than one larva is called *larvae.*

life cycle (LIFE sye-kuhl) *noun* the series of changes a living thing goes through from birth to death

M

maggot (MAH-gut) *noun* a worm-like thing that hatches from the eggs of flies

meteorologist (MEE-tee-ur-OL-oh-just) *noun* an expert in the weather

ME (EM-ee) *noun* a medical doctor who investigates suspicious deaths. It's short for *medical examiner.*

microscope (MYE-kruh-skope) *noun* a tool that makes things look bigger than they are. It's used to see details of small things.

P

pathologist (pah-THOL-oh-jist) *noun* a scientist who is an expert in diseases

PMI (PEE-em-eye) *noun* the time between when a person dies and when their body is discovered. It's short for *postmortem interval*.

postmortem interval (POHST-more-tehm IN-ter-vul) *noun* the time between when a person dies and when the body is discovered. The abbreviation is *PMI*.

preserve (pri-ZURV) *verb* to stay the same; to keep from decaying

prosecutor (PROSS-uh-kyoo-tur) *noun* a lawyer who represents the government in criminal trials. A prosecutor tries to prove that the person on trial is guilty.

pupa (PYOO-puh) *noun* the form of an insect in which the insect changes inside the cocoon. The insect emerges from the cocoon as an adult. More than one pupa is *pupae*.

pupal casing (PYOO-puhl CAY-sing) *noun* the empty cocoon that a pupa is in and an adult comes out of

pupate (PYOO-payt) *verb* to change into an adult

S

sickle (SIK-uhl) *noun* a farming tool with a rounded, sharp blade

specimen (SPESS-uh-muhn) *noun* a sample of something

suspect (SUHS-pekt) *noun* a person who might be guilty of a crime

T

TOD (TEE-oh-dee) *noun* the date and time when someone died. It's short for *time of death*.

toxicologist (TOK-sik-ohl-oh-jist) *noun* someone who studies poison

trowel (TROU-ul) *noun* a hand tool with a small, flat blade

V

victim (VIK-tuhm) *noun* a person who has been hurt or killed or made to suffer in some way

Index

Author's Note

If you Google the term *forensic entomology*, you'll find that you get more than 120,000 results! That's not a typo! There are tons of books, Web sites, and articles about this awesome science. There are even Web rings where you can get in touch with other people who are interested in it. It may be a creepy crawly topic, but there is plenty of information out there about it.

When reading or writing about real-life stuff, be sure to check your facts! In the process of writing this book, I found that books, Web sites, and articles didn't always agree with each other. One would have a piece of information that I thought was interesting or useful. But, when I compared it to another source, sometimes the information was slightly different. To be certain something is a fact, use many sources. And, more important, use trustworthy sources. Books and articles by the top experts or well-known news writers are a safe bet.

But be careful about trusting the Internet too much. All Internet sites are not created equal, and some aren't even factual! Anyone can post information on the Web. It doesn't mean that it is all well-researched or even true.

Check out the Resources section of this book for some of the most helpful sites and books. They'll give you the *real* lowdown on bug detectives.

ACKNOWLEDGEMENTS

I would like to thank the scientists who contributed to this book: Dr. Richard Merritt and Dr. John Wallace. Their time, effort, and expertise were invaluable to its creation. I would also like to thank Kate Waters, Suzanne Harper, Jennifer Wilson, Elizabeth Ward, and Katie Marsico for their support.

SOURCES

Richard W. Merritt, PhD, Michigan State University, contributor
John R. Wallace, PhD, Millersville University, contributor
Case #2: *A Fly for the Prosecution: How Insect Evidence Helps Solve Crimes*, M. Lee Goff
Case #3: *Death's Acre: Inside the Legendary Forensic Lab the Body Farm, Where the Dead Do Tell Tales*, Dr. Bill Bass and Jon Jefferson
Concept adviser: Robert D. Hall, PhD, JD, Associate Vice Chancellor for Research and Director of Compliance, Office of Research, University of Missouri